Rookie
Read-About® Science

Tiny Life in Your Home

By Lisa Trumbauer

Consultants
Reading Adviser
Nanci Vargus, EdD
Assistant Professor of Literacy
University of Indianapolis
Indianapolis, Indiana

Subject Adviser
Howard A. Shuman, PhD
Department of Microbiology
Columbia University Medical Center
New York, New York

Children's Press®
A Division of Scholastic Inc.
New York   Toronto   London   Auckland   Sydney
Mexico City   New Delhi   Hong Kong
Danbury, Connecticut

Designer: Herman Adler Design
Photo Researcher: Caroline Anderson
The photo on the cover shows bacteria, yeast, and fungus on a kitchen sponge.

Library of Congress Cataloging-in-Publication Data

Trumbauer, Lisa, 1963–
   Tiny life in your home / by Lisa Trumbauer ; consultant, Nanci R. Vargus.
     p. cm. — (Rookie read-about science)
   Includes index.
   ISBN 0-516-25274-7 (lib. bdg.)   0-516-25477-4 (pbk.)
   1. Microbiology—Juvenile literature. 2. Microbial ecology—Juvenile
literature. 3. Housing and health—Juvenile literature. I. Vargus, Nanci
Reginelli. II. Title. III. Series.
   QR57.T78 2005
   579'.17554—dc22   2005004631

CHILDREN'S PRESS, and ROOKIE READ-ABOUT®,
and associated logos are trademarks and/or registered trademarks
of Scholastic Library Publishing. SCHOLASTIC and associated logos
are trademarks and/or registered trademarks of Scholastic Inc.

1 2 3 4 5 6 7 8 9 10 R 14 13 12 11 10 09 08 07 06 05

Many kinds of life are
in your home. Some you
can see.

Some you cannot see.

Where are they?
They are everywhere!

Some are too small to see
with your eyes. Thousands
of tiny life forms could fit
on a pencil point.

6

Bacteria (bak-TIHR-ee-uh) are one kind of tiny life.

Bacteria need to eat and breathe, just like you.

Bacteria really like kitchens. Some bacteria like to eat food that people eat, such as fruits and vegetables.

Do you see the brown spots on the apples?

These brown spots mean the food has spoiled, or gone bad. Bacteria turns the fruit brown.

Some bacteria like to eat meat juices.

If juice spills on a counter, bacteria start to eat the meat juice. The bacteria could make you sick.

13

14

Some bacteria like warm things, such as warm apples and warm meat. They like warm air.

People put food in refrigerators. The food lasts longer here.

You can kill bad bacteria by cleaning.

Washing your hands
with soap and water
kills bacteria, too.

Not all bacteria are bad.
Some bacteria are good.
One kind of good bacteria
turns milk into yogurt.

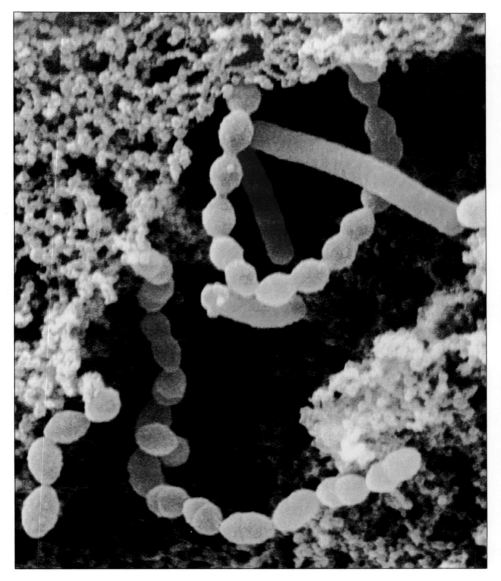

19

Do you like to eat cheese?

Cheese is made from milk. Bacteria helps turn milk into cheese.

Mold is tiny life, too. Mold may live in your home. It can grow on bread. Mold is a tiny life you can see.

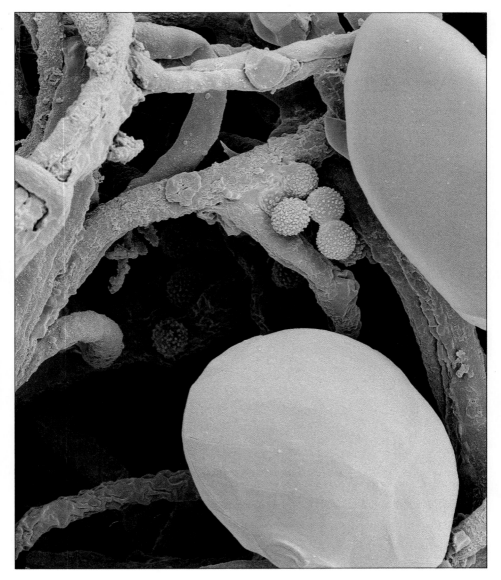

23

Mildew (MIL-doo) is another kind of tiny life. It grows in damp places. You can sometimes see mildew in the shower.

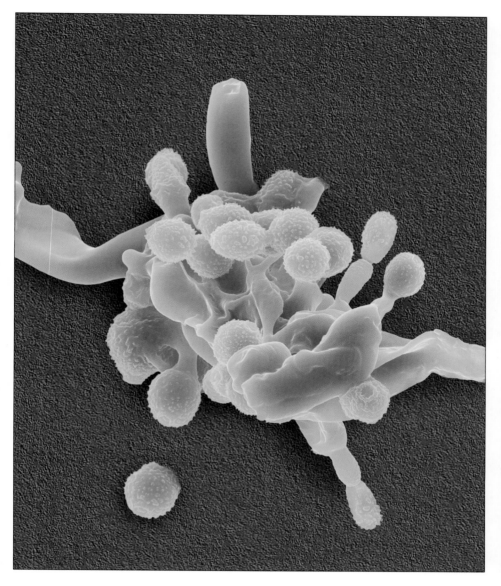

Fungus is another kind of tiny life. Yeast is a fungus. It eats sugar in bread dough. Yeast makes bread rise, or get fluffy.

Most kinds of tiny life are hard to see. Even so, they are still there.

They think your home is a good place to live, just like you do.

Words You Know

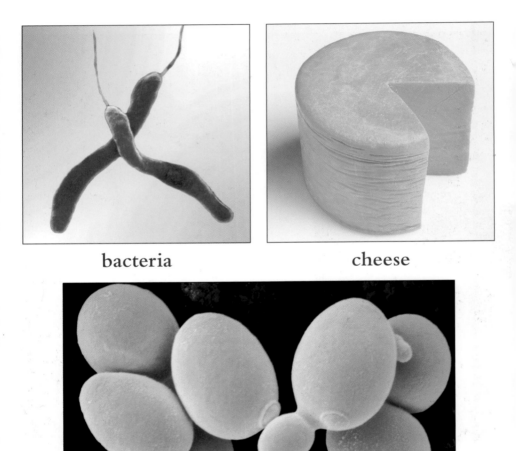

bacteria

cheese

fungus

kitchen

mildew

mold

yogurt

Index

About the Author

Lisa Trumbauer is the author of more than two hundred books for children, many of which are science-related. Formerly an editor with Scientific American Library, Ms. Trumbauer has edited several science programs for early learners. In addition, she has written science books about animals, plants, Earth, and the physical sciences. Ms. Trumbauer and her husband, Dave, live in New Jersey with their dog, Blue, and their cats, Cosmo and Cleo.

Photo Credits

Photographs © 2005: Corbis Images/Ariel Skelley: 3; Ellen B. Senisi: 13; Envision Stock Photography Inc./Osentoski & Zoda: 20, 30 top right; Getty Images/David Buffington/Photodisc Green: 5; ImageState: 16 (Banana Stock), 10 (EPC Photography); Peter Arnold Inc./Andreas Buck: 26; Photo Researchers, NY: 23 (Dr. Gary Gaugler), 22, 31 bottom left (Cordelia Molloy), 19, 27, 30 bottom (SciMAT); PhotoEdit: 9 (Tony Freeman), 14 (David Young-Wolff); Phototake/Dennis Kunkel: cover, 25; Stone/Getty Images: 24, 31 top right (Julia Fullerton-Batten), 18, 31 bottom right (Josh Mitchell), 29, 31 top left (Paul Redman); Visuals Unlimited: 6, 30 top left (Dr. Stanley Flegler), 17 (Mediscan).